The Labyrinth of Life

A Philosophical Perspective

DAN M. KHANNA

Copyright © 2015 Dan M. Khanna

All rights reserved.

ISBN: 0692389741
ISBN-13: 978-0692389744

DEDICATION

To all the kind, wonderful people, known and unknown, who visited my life, enriched me, mentored me, guided me, encouraged me, supported me, opened doors for me, and pointed me in the right direction selflessly with love.

My sincere gratitude, for without those simple sincere people my life journey would not be adventurous, fulfilling and rewarding. They are in my heart, my thoughts and in my dreams.

They are always with me.

CONTENTS

Prologue – Learning Life's Lessons

Reflections of a Writer - Writers and
    Poets: The Creative Process

The Karmic Journey	1
The Storm	5
The Spring of Discontent	7
The Mystery Called Life	8
The Pendulum Swings	10
Standing on the Cliff	12
In Search of Man	14
The Treasure Beneath	15
The Sunrise	18
Dare to Dream	20
Friends! Where are They?	22
As Time Goes By	23
Dashing the Dreams	25
Dreams Die Hard	26
The Lonely Statesman	27
The Price of Freedom	28
The Story of Life	29
Threading the Needle	31
Victory and Defeat	33
The Cracked Chalice	35
Chopping Life	37
The Bleeding Stone	38
The Relic	39
The Illusion of Happiness	40
The World I Life In	41
A Child Without Hope	42
Selling the Soul	43
The Robotic Life	44
An Ordinary Life	45
The Prisoner of Society	47
Exist to Exist	48

A Beautiful Life	49
What is Death?	50
The Dice of Life	51
The Edge of the Universe	52
The Fork in the Road	54
Wrong Turn	55
Two Lives	57
The Wrong Turn	58
The End of the Line	60
Passing Life	62
The End of a Journey	63
Life is an Experiment	64
The Last Throw	65
The Beautiful Life	66
To Live with Oneself	67
Peeling the Layers	68
The Damaged Goods	69
Window of Opportunity	70
The Illusion of Happiness	71
The Faith	72
God and I	73
In God's Hand	74
Life's Lessons	75
I Have to Accept	78
Accept the Consequences	81
The Summer of Discontent	82
The Twilight Zone	84
The Dawn of End	85
The Last Lap	87
The Ancient	89
The Final Exit	91
Exit Gracefully	92

THE STORM

It comes
With ferocity
That shakes the earth.

A battle
Between wind and earth
The eternal struggle
Between good and evil
Change and stability
Like life
Which struggles
To maintain
And change.

The storm
Brings force
To shake the foundation
Of existence
Of what is there
And what it
Likes to carve.

Force and power
The energy
That drives civilizations
Sometimes to doom
Is needed
To move ahead
To shake the present
For the future.

It is turbulence
That drives civilizations
To achieve
What it truly is

A place which can survive anything
Or a place
Which comes apart
At the seams.

The storm hits us all
In life
In nature
In world.

It is part of the universe
A part of existence.

Whether one survives
The storm
Depends on what one learns
Resilience
And the ability
To weather the storm
And change.

THE SPRING OF DISCONTENT

Spring is here
flowers are blooming
time to plant new seeds
but, there is discontent
in my life
which does not want
to plant
the seeds of failure
but stare
at the barren trees of fall

wondering
why leaves fall
and raking the leaves of life
into bags
to throw away
ignoring the birth of spring

ignoring life
refusing to blossom
and refusing to plant new seeds
that is
the spring of discontent.

THE MYSTERY CALLED LIFE

Is life a mystery?
In many ways, it is.
Are we a mystery?
Maybe, we are.
When innocent people
Get ravaged by the storm
To lose everything they have
Why them?
Why at all?
Nature
Powerful
Unpredictable
Comes in all forms
Earthquakes, volcanoes, hurricanes, disease
Why?
Is it the price of living on this planet?
A ball
Out in the wilderness of the universe
Rotating and revolving
In space
By forces
It does not control
Just like us
Who have no control
Over the forces of nature
And over our earth
Just rotating and revolving
At the whim of an unknown force
Tumbling and regrouping
To stand
To stand still
To stand and walk
To walk, where?

For all directions
Reach someplace
We travel
We return
We go up
We come down
The forces around us
Envelop us
Why?
What do we do?
We fight humanity
To feel that we are powerful
Against natural forces
We kill our own kind
To prove ourselves
But powerful against what?
While we kill our own kind
Nature kills us
Reminding us
That we are weak and vulnerable
But do we learn?
No
That is a mystery
The inability of humans
To learn from nature
To behave in a manner
That enhances humankind
But we degrade humankind
And nature
Continues to train us
Trust us
Nurture us, nourish us
But, we go on
Without fathoming
The true nature of life and the universe
That is a mystery
And, it will
Remain a mystery.

THE PENDULUM SWINGS

The pendulum swings
Between life and death
And at each end
It pauses
To decide where to go.

But, does it really decide?
Or, is it forced to decide?
Or, the decision is made already
By the forces of the universe?

For it swings again
Not knowing when to stop
For it, the stop
Means the end of life
The end of its rhythm
But not its purpose
Which is to swing
Between life and death.

It swings
Because of nature.
It reverses
Because of nature.
Why it does that
Only nature knows.

But it swings
In perpetual motion
To the rhythm of life
Or to the rhythm of death
For eventually
They are the same.

The pendulum swings
To keep alive
And to let nature
Decide when it should stop.

STANDING ON THE CLIFF

As I stand on the edge
At the precipice of life
I see the ocean below me
Hammering at the cliff.

The waves beckon me
With undulating rhythm.

I admire the beauty
Though dangerous it is.
Beauty can be dangerous.
I like the scene
But am afraid of its force.
To be with the waves
Is tempting
To get there
Is hazardous.

I am there
And not there.
I am at the edge
Looking below
At the sea
Trying to carve a hole
In the cliff.

The gust of wind
Shakes my thoughts
And carries me
Towards the waves.

Will I fall?
Will I soar?

Will it push me
Into the depths of the ocean
Or slam me against the life?
Or will it carry me
Above the water
Into the sky
To distant lands
And ancient worlds?

What should I do?
Fight the wind
And stay on the edge
Or let me be carried
At the whim of the wind.
Let the force of destiny
Guide me.
Take me
To the ocean
Or to the sky.

Do I know?
Do I care?
I have reached the edge
Of cliff
Of life
I got there
Now I am here.

Let the force of nature
Decide my next move.

I wait
For the next gust of wind
And let myself
Be at the mercy of the wind.
Wherever it takes me
Is my world
My new world.
My new home.

IN SEARCH OF MAN

Where is man?
It is not the many faces
That walks gloomily in the street.

Where is man?
It is not that exists and survives
In the tyranny of the few.

Where is man?
It is not that exists passively
To let others do his thinking.

Where is man?
That was supposed to think
And create a world of joy and happiness.

Where is man?
It is not the same person
That rapes the place it lives in.

Where is man?
It is not the same person
That differentiates, rebukes and kills.

Where is man?
That was supposed to
Create a heaven on earth.

We live around men,
But, there are no men.
We still
Search for man.

THE TREASURE BENEATH

The treasures
Are hidden
In dungeons
Beneath the sea
In deep caves
And mysterious caverns
We hunt them
To enrich ourselves
To get us out
Of our present
Leaving a world of
Fame and fortune
To be loved
And be respected
For our outward show
Affluence and ornamental structures
It is a show
Of hollowness
For the treasure we seek
Is within us
It is our foundation
That we weaken
By building
Elaborate structures
That portray
What we are not
And hide
What is within
It is a structure
To impress the world
But not ourselves

As time goes on
We build more structures

More ornaments
And further
Weaken our foundation
Ourselves
'Til we are
A huge building
A giant structure, hollow inside
That is about to crumble
Then we prop it up
With more structures
To secure
Weaknesses
To discover one day
That we are in an empty building
Alone and lost
Trying to find
A way out
The process starts
Tearing down
All walls
All structures
To strip ourselves
Of the exterior
To search the interior
Of our ourselves
To start with the
Foundation
Of our heart and soul
Of our responsibility
To ourselves
That we need to build
It is ourselves that needs love

It is ourselves
That needs cultivation
It is ourselves
That needs growth
We start at the basics
Just like kids
At the first day of school

Learn, to grow
To build ourselves
As humans with soul
With spirit
With energy
With love
To create
A foundation
And a structure
That is lasting
That is our treasure
It's the treasure,
The treasure beneath.

THE SUNRISE

The first rays
Of light and hope
Escape the darkness
To reveal a new day
That is emerging
To seek a new beginning
Of hope and faith
To start a new day
That will change everything
Or change nothing

Will it be a day
That propels my life
In new directions
Or, will it be a day
That will fade away
Like other days
That I don't care to remember
Just a day
In the life of life

But, then it is sunrise
The rays brighten the sky
The shiny golden rays
That emit
A desire of hope
For a better world
A peaceful world
With no violence

As we awake
We are full of hopes
And then the reality of existence hits us

And we become robots
Just going around in circles
Trodding the earth
That supports us
The rays brighter the world
But our lives remain in the darkness
Still awaiting sunrise
The sunrise of our world.

DARE TO DREAM

I dream
When I am awake
I dream
When I am asleep
I dream
Of a life
That I should have
I dream
Of a life
That I deserve
I dream
Of a love
That I should have.

But, then
Dreams are dreams
Do they come true?
I don't know.
But, dreams are fun
They give you comfort
Hope for the future
Maybe, some of them
Will come true
That will be good
Dreams are us
We must dream
For without dreams
We are empty shells
Just caricatures
Dreams make us humans
They propel us forward
We must not give up

Dreams can become reality
They do
Dream
Dare to dream.

FRIENDS! WHERE ARE THEY?

I hope
that after my death
I don't have any friends.

For in this life
Friends have just hurt.

They gloat
on your failures.
Delight
in your suffering.
Envy
your joy.
Stab you
in your back.
Compliment
when they don't mean it.
Sympathize
with joy.

In time
As it does happen
You lose your friends.
We become alone
As we
were destined to be.

Friends are rare
If you find one.
Friends!
Where are you?

AS TIME GOES BY

As time goes by
It becomes cruel
And a blessing
The friends that we grew up with
Become strangers
Not necessarily by choice
Some by distance
Some by marriage
Some by life
Some by wisdom
Interests change
Lifestyles change
We still keep in touch
With some childhood friends
Not for friendship
More for nostalgia
To reflect on
The good old days
That makes us feel good.

But, time has passed
We are in different time zones
The world is same or new
Depends on how you look at it
We have new friends
More for socializing
Than for soul-searching
The truth of the past
Is replaced by
Artificiality of belonging
Priorities change

We are no longer
On the list of calls
Our thinking has changed

Loneliness
Wants friendships
That are no longer there
It is best
To reflect on the good times
Fond memories
Happy events
And bury them
In the heart
And move on
With a smile
On our lips
The past is over
Time has passed
And it is
A new time.

DASHING THE DREAMS

The dreams that I had
As a young boy
Dreams of a future
Idealism of innocence
Creating a perfect world in the mind
A Utopian existence
Of a lovely home
Partner and family
A settled secure life
Great dreams, great expectations
But the dreams dashed
Like the waves
That dash against the rocks
Scattering and disillusioned
Dismayed and destroyed.

But dreams never die
Just like the waves
They keep on coming
Pounding relentlessly on the rocks
'Til it starts chipping it away
Slowly eroding the barriers
Then one wave
Lifts the rock
And hurls it away
Clearing the path for dreams
To advance and make a beached
On the shores of life
Dreams may dash
But they do not die
The power of dreams
Builds future.

DREAMS DIE HARD

There are dreams
And there are
Dreams of dreams
Dreams of a life
That one wants to live
A life that fulfills us
Our dreams are born
When we are young
We observe the world
And our innocent minds
Create visions
Of the world we want to live in
Simple and uncluttered
Peace and contentment
And happiness forever
But life is not like that
It plunders your soul
As it grinds you
The dreams become ashes
But in the ashes
There is still a spark
A smoldering spark
That is ready to ignite
And erupt into a bright flame
That lights the world
Telling the world
That I am alive
And ready to take on
Every challenge, every hindrance
For dreams are real
And I have
Dared to dream.

THE LONELY STATESMAN

The lonely statesman
Is a noble soul
Trying to find some sense
In a distorted world
Straightening pieces
That are crooked and broken
As he struggles alone
In a world full of people
Yet very alone
To leave a mark
On an erasable life
To be forgotten
In the pages
Of a desolate history book
And such is the life
Of a lonely statesman.

THE PRICE OF FREEDOM

Freedom is a right
That we all have and must retain
And pay any price
Go keep it
For it is the only right
Worth defending
And paying with life
If it so demands
For no life is worth living
Without freedom
But freedom
Must be tempered with
Responsibility and dignity
Respect for other freedoms
And dignity of acceptance
Only then is freedom
Really a freedom.

THE STORY OF LIFE

It was a life once
Of happiness
Of future
Of hope of dreams.

Then came a storm
A violent storm
Uprooting trees
Destroying hopes.

And then it was over
A barren land
Devoid of life.
No water
No flowers
An arid land
That needed to bloom again.

There was earth.
There was soil.
There was water.
That's all one needs
For a beginning.

A beginning
Of new hopes
Of new life
Of new world.

A land
That is carved
Out of nothing
Is a land
That is beautiful.

It is you.
You made it.
It is yours
To nurture
And grow
To make it
Into a paradise
Where
Life blooms.

THREADING THE NEEDLE

Threading the needle
Is an art
That I have not mastered
I can see the hole in the needle
I hold the thread in my hand
But when they come together
My hand shakes
I miss
Again and again
I steady myself
Thin the thread
Still I miss
I wish the hole were bigger
But the mirage
Keeps separating the alignment
I miss again and again
Just like my life
I can see it
But, I keep passing it by
So close
Yet so far
I see it
And I don't see it
Like my life
Happiness and living
Is life
Trying to thread
Happiness through life
But, it just misses
Again and again

So I begin again
With hope and confidence
Trying to thread the needle again.

VICTORY AND DEFEAT

I win, I lose
My life stares at me
Wondering, what am I doing?
Peeking at the past
Or, gazing at the future
Even I don't know
What I am doing?
I have been a victor
I have been defeated
The ups and downs of life
Have eroded the differences
Between victory and defeat
To me now
They are two sides
Of the same coin
The lashings of life
Have welted my skin
To the point
That it has hardened
Into a protective covering
That makes victory or defeats the same
I can't tell the difference
The emotional exuberance
Is the same
The thrill is the same
The agony is the same
In one sense
It is just my life
A life of undulating curves
That propels forward
At uneven speeds
To jolt me

And remind me
That victory and defeat
Are the same.

THE CRACKED CHALICE

I hold a chalice
With the elixir of life in it
That I want to drink
And be alive again
But I notice a crack
A gentle crack
That extends from the base
To the rim
I stare at it
To see if it will hold the elixir
Or, let it seep through the crack
I hold the chalice tenderly
Not trying to grasp
And break the chalice
For I like the chalice
It has beauty
It has curves
It has character
It proudly exhibits the crack
For the crack is part of it
It gives it dignity
A flawed beauty
That makes the chalice
A unique vessel
That holds elixir
Hope for people
As I lift it to my lips
The eternity passes
I savor the elixir
The crack has made it sweeter

I drink, I savor
I am alive
My love
The cracked chalice.

CHOPPING LIFE

The woodcutter
Looks at the tree
That stands inert
Full of leaves and strong branches
Ready to receive the blows without a fight
The woodcutter
Sizes the enemy
Picks the ax
And strikes a blow
The tree stiffens
A silent scream
As pain runs through the roots
Wondering
What it has done
It grew from a small seed
Provided shade to travelers
Provided fruits for the hungry
Provided flowers for beauty
But, today
It stands helpless
As blows strike it mercilessly
Its branches fall painfully
Soon it is stripped of all dignity
It stands bare
Without branches and flowers
As its trunk is cut
Exposing roots
'Til no life remains
To be hauled and burnt
For reasons
That it doesn't understand
But, its life is over
And it ceases to exist
As we humans
End our lives
Chopping trees.

THE BLEEDING STONE

The stone
That bleeds tears
Is my heart
A pulsating emotion
That crashed into a meteorite
Instantly turning into a molten stone
That bleeds at will
As it gets kicked and thrown
To fall with pain
On a cruel surface
Shrieking a silent scream
That no one hears
It sits alone
Waiting for the next kick
Waiting for someone
To pick up
And throw far away
To be picked up again
Maybe, the stone is unique
It has a personality
That someone will hold it
Caress it
And take it
For a collector item
To sit alone
Among other stones
Reflecting how it got there
Bleeding tears
Of joy and sorrow
Staying still
In perpetual stillness
To be forgotten forever.

THE RELIC

The relic
Is a person of life
That came and went
Leaving impressions
Of a forgotten past
That believed in love
To realize
That love was just grains of sand
That left you
When you held it tight
Relic of the past
That believed in integrity
Your word was your bond
Their word was a word
Faith and trust.

But now
The relic stands alone
Staring at the empty statues
Of faith and trust
The hollowness of integrity
As survival and selfishness
Lies and deceit
Make your innocence a crime
An ancient structure
To be admired and forgotten
An ancient person
In a modern world
Lost and forgotten
To be remembered
As a lost art
Presented in exhibitions
As a relic
To be admired from the distance.

THE ILLUSION OF HAPPINESS

The illusion of happiness
Is a dangerous mirage
That feels like an oasis
Yet it is a barren desert
Ready to swallow you
In its quicksand
While you cling
To an image of
Paradise
That exists only
In your mind
While the reality hits you
Like a jackhammer
Bringing you to your senses
That happiness is just a dream
It does happen
When it does
But mostly
Happiness is just an illusion.

THE WORLD I LIVE IN

The world I live in
Seems ancient and alien.

The life that I live
Seems struggle and survival.

The people that I live with
Seem callous and cruel.

The friends that I live with
Seem indifferent and indignant.

The relatives that I deal with
Seem dangerous and demanding.

The lovers that I live with
Seem separate and selfish.

The children I live with
Seem carefree and careless.

The God that I worship
Seems ignorant and impotent.

I will soon pass from this world
The world that I live in

But the world will go on
And on, and on, and on.

A CHILD WITHOUT HOPE

A child without hope
Is a dead child
A child with hope
Is an unborn child
A child without opportunity
Is a lifeless child
Whose life died before birth
But that child is born
Somewhere every second
Without any hope of making it in the world
Without any future
It is a curse on mankind
That allows this to happen
Yet we live and ignore
What that child should do
We are incensed with our lives
Ignoring the future
Of innocent lives
Brought into this world
Through sex, lust or love
But not giving that spark
That propels and prepares
The child for the future
A future
In which the child
Creates a new world
Of love, hope and success
It is a disgrace
For humankind
To not let every child
Have an opportunity
To make a new world every child deserves
A better future
Than we had
It is a child with hope.

SELLING THE SOUL

I had a soul
That I sold
For a pittance
To live
In a materialistic world
Where only money matters
Everything has
A monetary value
Even life
Even values
Even souls
Us humans too
We think
Of self-interest first
And what is in it for me today
We sell our souls
Everyday
For instant gratification
For selfish motives
The soul becomes a commodity
To be bought and sold
Just like
Goods in a marketplace
The divine soul
Is just a good
With a price
The decline of humankind
Like a sunset
As the sun
Is swallowed
By the sea.

THE ROBOTIC LIFE

We wake up
Go to work
Do our job
Return home
Do our routines
Watch television
Spend time with family or friends
Eat and sleep
To start the routine
Yes, we have our hobbies
Our interests
We have vacations
We attend parties
And then
All that becomes
A routine
A habit
Just like a robot
Living a robotic life.

AN ORDINARY LIFE

I lead
A very ordinary life
I go to work
In a mediocre line of work
Pay the bills
Watch television and movies
For entertainment
See few friends occasionally
I cook to survive
I pay my taxes
Help government
Off my back
I vote most of the time
As a good citizen
To participate
In our political process
Knowing well
That it does not matter
What I vote
What I think
I am a non-entity
Just an ordinary citizen
Who makes this country run
It may be a boring life
But because of me
And many other ordinary citizens
This country is great
For we do our duty
We do our work
We know that our names
May not appear in local obituaries
But, that does not matter

For we made this country run
And made it a better place
We are simple
We are ordinary
Our lives are ordinary
But, we are special.

THE PRISONER OF SOCIETY

The world is a prison
We leave only on death
The society is our prison
Telling us what to do
Telling us what to think
To create living robots
Draped in mediocrity
Living uneventful lives
And hoping
That we will be mentioned
In our local obituary
That our society values
Only few make it there
The rest just pass
Into a better world
Escaping a society
That is just a prison.

EXIST TO EXIST

I live
Actually I exist
I go through the motions of life
I go to work
Where it is just work
To get paid
So I can take care of basic needs
Yes, I have desires
But my meager sustenance
Negates any desires
Yes, I have dreams
But they remain dreams
For existence takes all energy away
I become a robot
Going through the motions
Of living each day
Bringing me closer to the end
Wondering is this all to life
Oh, yes
I wanted more
But the hurricanes of life
Leveled all hopes
The loves vanished
'Til life became mere existence
Now I exist to exist.

A BEAUTIFUL LIFE

Is life beautiful?
Yes, it is
Look around
See and feel the nature
The myriads of colors
The natural
Carving oceans and mountains
The running rivers
The innocent splendor of animals
The towering trees
The velour valleys
Yes, life is beautiful
And then we have
Humans
That defile a beautiful life
And destroy nature
In the name of progress
They kill their own earth
To survive and grow
And destroy
A beautiful life.

WHAT IS DEATH?

What is death?
It is not the end of life
For life can end
Many times before death
People stop living
When they become
Pawns of the society
Existing for the sake of existence
Without laughter or passion
Each day is just another day
Going through routine
Just to kill the day
That is not life
Life without living
Is death of life
You have died
While living
And that is
Real death.

THE DICE OF LIFE

Life is a gamble
We are dealt cards
That we need to live with
We throw dice
Hoping to win
But, it is a chance
We gamble our lives
On opportunities and hope
Dreaming of dreams
Throwing dice with the hope
That it will be the last throw

You bet it all
Pray, and throw the dice
You close your eyes
To make a final wish
It will be all or nothing
You will get what you want
Or walk away alone and lonely
As an empty loser
But, one must try
To test fate
And bet it all
On one throw
The last dice of life.

THE EDGE OF THE UNIVERSE

I stand at the
Edge of the universe
Gazing at our world
That spins rhythmically.
I see it
But I am not part of it
For I was thrown off
Our world
A long time ago
Hurled into space
To the end of the universe
Where one world ends
And another begins
It is an edge
That separated the past from the future
It is a chance
To observe oneself
In the grand scheme of things
Where I stand
Where I fit
Did I ever fit?
I am here alone
Surrounded by worlds
That are moving in all directions
Am I moving with them?
Or do I just see them passing by?
Am I part of them?
Or am I just an observer?
Will I move with them?
Or, be left behind?
I don't know.

I am a bystander
Waiting for the Divine Hand
To show me the path
Which I must travel
Alone with someone
Which road to take?
Where will it lead?
Where will it end?
Will it end
Or, will it go on forever?
Questions?
But no answers.
Answers elude me
But the view is magnificent
It is all there
Good and bad
Happy and sad
Beauty and ugly
But it is there.
I stand and look
And wonder
When will I be part of this universe?
This world?
Or will I remain an outsider?
A bystander
On the edge
Of the universe.

THE FORK IN THE ROAD

The crossroads of life
Stands empty
Desolate and barren
I stand alone
Beaten by hot desert wind
What to do?
Where to go?
So many paths
Leading in so many directions
All shrouded with dust
With no visible end
I have to move
I have to travel
Pick a road
I seek
Heavenly guidance
None is there
I toss my fate to the winds
And take a road
Not knowing where it will go
Where it will end
But, I must travel as life demands
And trust fate
My past determines my future
I am on a path
That will determine my future
My destiny
I must accept.

WRONG TURN

Sometime, somewhere
In my life
I took a wrong turn
That took me
On journeys
That I had not planned
For all my plans
Went into disarray
And each plan
Resulting in new plans
All plans
Falling by the wayside.

My life took a turn of its own
Unknown to me and to my life
I traveled on journeys
That crisscrossed
Continents
Into unchartered waters
Wandering into an open sea
With no land in sight
Depending on intuition
To guide my soul.

My journey became turbulent
As waves crested me
And drowned me
Like a roller coaster
Got tossed around
At its whims and moods
And that ups and downs
Seem flat to me

I had no idea
Where I was being lead.
I drifted with a purpose
To find land
Where I could stand
And find my path.

Should I seek my original path?
Or find a new path
To unknown new places?

But the wrong turn
Has wasted so much of my life
Or has it enriched me
With the lessons of life
To prepare me for a new journey.

Have I learned, or
I just felt lost.
It depends
On how I view my life
Whether the wrong turn
Was a mistake, or
Divine guidance
Only time will tell.

But, I have ways to go
To learn
Whether the wrong turn
Was self-inflicted, or
A Divine nudge.
'Til then
I just go on
The path
Of the wrong turn.

TWO LIVES

We live
Two lives
One for existence
One for our dreams
They are like
The two tracks of the train
Parallel, together and alone
Existing for a purpose
To hold a life
That travels on its shoulders
Towards unknown destination
Never merging
Never becoming one
The dream and reality
The two anchors of life.

THE WRONG TRAIN

I had to make a journey
A journey of life
I arrive at the station
Ask the conductor
For the right train
I know my destination
I board the train
The journey starts
I see fellow travelers
All around me
The train gallops
And soon
The past is gone
The future comes
Bearing down on you
The station comes
It doesn't look familiar
You were on the wrong train
You trusted the conductor
What do you do?
You search the faces
Of fellow travelers
Some smile, some frown
Some turn away
Who do you ask?
You trust Fate
Maybe, the new destination
Is the right one
Or should you go to the next station
And find another train

But, how do you know
That the next station
Is the right place to step down
Maybe, the trains there
Take you in another direction
You sit, you wait
The train thunders on
You are surrounded by strangers
All cheering your wasteful journey
The end comes, you are there
The destination, not what you wanted
But, it is home
The price of the wrong train.

THE END OF THE LINE

The train stops
It is the last station
It is the end of the line
I have to get off
I have no choice
I want to go further
But, I can't
I wonder what I will see
When I get off
Has my journey stopped?
Journeys of life
Do not stop
They halt
Or get derailed
But, do not stop
I have to leave the train
I step out of the train
Seeking exit
To a place that I don't know
Searching for a familiar face
To give me direction
But, I am alone
All directions
Seem the same to me
They all lead everywhere and nowhere
With just my instinct and destiny
To guide me
I venture out
To bright sunshine
Amidst strangers
To search for a new train

That will continue my journey
To unknown destination
'Til it comes
To the end of its line.

PASSING LIFE

As I stand at the zenith of my life
I see it passing by me
I gaze at it
Wondering if this life is mine
It looks familiar
I was on it once
Now I wave at it
As it pulls away from me
Hoping it will recognize me
And stop to let me get on it
But it ignores my gestures
And moves on
While I stand alone
With a raised hand.

THE END OF A JOURNEY

The train stops
It is the last station
I have to get off
Pick up my baggage
Disembark
And search for an exit
It was a nice journey
Great sights, boring sights
Mountains and rivers
Plains and fields
All with their own beauty
But the journey is over
As I exit into a new city
I wonder what will I find
Should I find a resting place
And call it quits
Or should I search for a new adventure
In a new place
For the journey
Never ends.

LIFE IS AN EXPERIMENT

Life is an experiment
We are brought into it
But are not taught
How to live in it
We try, we blunder
We make mistakes
We score victories
It is an endless
Series of experiments
Some win, some lose
But, we keep trying
For we are part of life
And we have to live it
We are lonely
We are novice
That is life
We are thrown into it
And we must learn
It is an experiment.

THE LAST THROW

The last throw of dice
On the gambling table of life
Is a daring challenge
Risking it all
On just one throw
To win or lose everything
The fate of life
Rests on this throw
Either walks away a winner
Or, a great loser
Sometimes
Life demands that of us
To risk it all
In a last throw.

THE BEAUTIFUL LIFE

Life is beautiful
If you want it to be
Life is hell
If you want it to be
But what you make of life
Is up to you
Of course
The Divine touch
Does help
Life is a necessity
To get out of this world
So live it
Make it beautiful
For it may be
The last chance
As you fade into oblivion
With just a memory.

TO LIVE WITH ONESELF

There is nothing harder
Than trying to live with oneself
For oneself is true
It tells the truth
It is honest
It is objective
It has no hidden agenda
It is your best friend
But we ignore it
For we are afraid of truth
It may tell us
What we don't want to hear
We are scared of it
For to be with oneself is pure
But we live in a contaminated world
So we ignore the truth
For an artificial world
For living with oneself
Is not easy.

PEELING THE LAYERS

Life is built by layers
Each layer enveloping an experience
That we go through
As we build our lives
Each layer shrouds us
Gives us a new experience
That shapes our perceptions of ourselves
Soon we are nothing except layers of life
That hide us
From our true selves
Then one day we look at ourselves in the mirror
And not see us
Just layers that cover us
We are aliens to ourselves
We start peeling the layers
One layer at a time
Slowly but surely
Not ready to shock ourselves
As layers come off
Just like a mask
The experiences come off
Exposing our real self
The innocent self
That created life and God
Trying to find the love of life
That was divine
But got covered with layers
The peeling goes on
'Til we are naked and done
All divine, all human
Our true self.

THE DAMAGED GOODS

The box
Sitting alone
Dented and damaged
Sides caved in
From transit
A lonely journey
It endured to reach its destination.

The box is me
Damaged goods
Scarred by life
Dented by emotions
Damaged by the world
As I tried to reach my destination.

Now I sit alone
Waiting for inspection
To see the extent of real damage
To fix what is broken
Or just pay out the insurance
But, I am damaged
Never to be whole again
Never to be perfect
I have to live with my fate
And accept the damage
Do what I can to continue my journey
Broken, but not defeated
For I am still a box
That contains me
I may be damaged
But, I am still alive.

WINDOW OF OPPORTUNITY

There is a small window
That remains shut most of the time
It is the window to watch
For it has the best view
It has fresh breeze
But we ignore it most of the time

For it is too small
The big windows offer great views
Of known scenes
The breeze is familiar
Easy to open
But it is the small window
That remains shut and stuck
For it opens doors to a world
A future that is ours
It is the window of opportunity
The only window that matters.

THE ILLUSION OF HAPPINESS

Happiness is a quest
For most of us
Hoping to find it
In our lifetime
Yes, we do touch upon it
From time to time
We are occasionally
Glazed by its kindness
But for most of us
Happiness remains an illusion
That tempts us
But never satisfies us
We grasp it
But come up with empty air
We lunge at it
And hit a brick wall
As we settle into a routine
Of survival
Trying to make a living
In a greedy world
Struggling to meet ends
With dreams of riches
That may never come out our way
Hoping that riches will lead to happiness
Another illusion
That will soon burst
And we will keep
Staring at the wilderness
Hoping to carve monuments
With imagination and hope
As we struggle through life
With an illusion of happiness.

THE FAITH

Faith is required
To make it through life
Faith in oneself
In God
In love
In our values
In others

These combinations of faith
Is essential for life
To make it through
With its ups and downs
With its good and bad
If you have faith
In yourself
That life is ordained
And God is watching over you
But it all will pass
One way or another
If you have faith
In yourself
And people
Who believe in you
For in the end
It is just you
And people
Who love you
Just thank them
You will succeed
Let faith guide you.

GOD AND I

God and I
Have a lovely relationship
He loves me
Protects me
Whenever I do something stupid
Yet He pounds me
When I do wrong
I like it that way
For I do love God
I know
I cannot do without Him
I remember
When I was down
He picked me up
When I was about to have an accident
He came to save me
A guardian angel
I know it was God
For only divine intervention
Could have protected me
The fatal illnesses
He carried me
Safely to safety
Yet, I question Him
Why am I here?
He tells me
You are my child
I love you
You will remain with Me
Forever
For I am your true friend
Who loves you unselfishly
Making you a better person
For you are Mine.

IN GOD'S HAND

The Hand of God
Holds me gently
Keeping me warm and comfortable
I am contented
I live a life
That pulls me in all directions
I don't know what to do
My plans don't work
My dreams crash
I just give up
Lost and confused
Then I look up
Seeking Divine guidance
That will hold my life
And guide me wisely
To whatever destination
God desires
I let myself go
I have to
For I have not done
A great job with my life
And I put myself
In God's Hand.

LIFE'S LESSONS

My life
What have I learned from it
As I enter the twilight of my life?

I reflect
The memories take me back
To my carefree youth
Under the love and guidance of my parents.

Then I was on my own
Living an adventurous life
Traveling through spaces
And strange lands
Searching for a dream
I may or may not find
The undulating plains
Throwing me up and down
Catching me
Propelling me up again
Holding me
When I fell
But, it was a good life
Will I change anything?
No
It was meant for me
And I have lived it with emotion
Good and bad
Happy and sad
Just like any other life
But, it was mine
As I see the end
I leave my thoughts
Of the lessons that I learned.

First, plans do not always work
Plan, but do not live by it
The frustration and disillusionment
May shatter your will
For will is strong
And you must have it
To endure your journey.

Second, not everything in life
Can be explained
Some things just happen
Some people we just meet
Some events just happen
Some episodes just appear
Accept it
Let it go
Do not analyze
Do not question
Do not question!
Just accept it
As a divine gift
That is what we are given
It is our path
Just learn and move on.

Third, our minds become destructive
It fails to reason
It shuts up
Justifying every thought and action
Our mind has taken over
We have exited our soul
We live in an artificial world
Leaving touch with reality
That is self-destructive.

Fourth, we must bear the responsibility of our decisions
Our actions
Not blame others
Not blame the system
Not blame life

Accept the consequences
Of your decisions
Learn to live with you
It is all you have
It will make you an emotionally richer human.

These are the lessons I share with the world around me
As I fade into oblivion
My life is lived
But the journey continues.

I HAVE TO ACCEPT

I have to accept
That I am alive against my wishes
I have to accept
That my dreams of childhood
Got scattered in the wind
As I stare at an empty wasteland

I have to accept
That my parents are not alive
To guide me and point me
In the right direction
As I flounder through life
Without their guidance and love

I have to accept
That I wasted my life
In frivolous pursuits
Of unreachable stars

I have to accept
That my health
Keeps knocking me down
While keeping me alive
As I await the inevitable

I have to accept
That I have no love in life
And I may remain loveless
Wanting love

I have to accept
That I live alone
In a desolate environment
Without friends or culture
Slowly withering away in life

I have to accept
That romance is just a dream
A wishful thinking
That once excited me
Now may remain dormant
Ready to explode anytime

I have to accept
That the end that I seek
May elude me against my wishes
And only come at its time
Not at my desire

I have to accept
That happiness is an illusion
That fleetingly touched me
And then vanished into thin air

I have to accept
That my life's journey will be alone
Searching for a place
That I would like to call home
But, I may never find it
And I may remain homeless
In my own home

I have to accept
My fate
My life
For it is God's will

And, I must accept
God's will.

ACCEPT THE CONSEQUENCES

I have no one to blame
For all the misadventures
In my life
Too bad it is an easy way out
But my life is my responsibility
Sure there are things
That I cannot control
But I am a product
Of my dreams and dilemmas
I am what I make myself
Good and bad
But in the end
It is my responsibility
I must assume and accept
The consequences.

THE SUMMER OF DISCONTENT

The time has come
To think of my life
As it nears a final closure
I wonder
Where am I?
What have I done?
It is a time for reflection
This summer
The summer of discontent
The restlessness
That permeates through me
The time has come
To rethink my life
And move to a new world
Where my past hopes
Will flourish
Where my lost dreams
Will be realized
Where I will find a home
My soul
And final resting place.
Where that is
I don't know
When will it happen?
I don't know
But, I know
That my time now
Has come to an end
Life and love
Are at crossroads
The past not very kind

The future
Beckons with open arms
To embrace me
In its bosom
To soothe me
To nurture my wounds
And bask me
In love and glory
And lay my head
In the pillow of God
Where I find myself
One with God
The finality to a life
That went astray
And must seek
Its end
In the palms
Of God.

THE TWILIGHT ZONE

The twilight of life
Has diminishing hopes
After a long existence.

The final sunset
Which has its best view,
For it is the last
That the eyes will see.

As the sun sinks,
So does life
Which the sun will never see again
For there is no sunrise.

A night of reflection
A night of remembrance
Of the first sunrise
Which was so beautiful.

But as the day wore on
The sun scorched life
Leaving memories
And a beautiful sunset of hopes
And dreams.

As I bid farewell
To the final sunset
The night approached
The final night
From which there is no sunrise.

It is the night of nights
The final end
The end of all ends
The twilight of life.

THE DAWN OF END

I am staring
At a brilliant dawn
Orange reddish
Rays streaming
Through the distant mountains
Bringing color
To scattered clouds
It is beautiful
Another day of hope
A new day
That tells me
That it is the start
Of my end
Ending a journey
That began at birth
It is the dawn of the end
It is so beautiful
Exhilarating and thrilling
I now know
That twilight will come
With the sunset
As the golden sun
Plunges into the ocean
Scattering the sky
With brilliant colors.

Will my end be like that?
Showering colors at the world
Or will my sun
Drown behind the clouds
For no one to see
Or experience my end
Just an end
That no one saw

But, the dawn was beautiful
It started the end
A glorious end.

THE LAST LAP

I am running
The last lap
Tired but determined
To not just complete it
For that I will
But with a victory
With my arms raised high
In thrill and exaltation
The cheering of crowds
The glory of the crown
That will be put on my head
I will bow gracefully
With humility
And reflect
On how I got there
Hard work
Determination
Perseverance
Endurance
The grinding of life
The mashing of stones
That crumbles us
Into sand like pieces
That may scatter
In the wind
But those specs
Are alive
They gather
Become a stone
Then a rock
A force
That hits hard
To shake the world
The ashes become a sphinx
Rising

To demonstrate
That there is still
Life left in me
That can
Take on any challenge
That fate hurls at me
I may be on
The last leg of life's journey
But there is still
Life left in me
A burst of energy
A desire to win
I will defeat life
Rise to the occasion
Take on the final challenge
I ran hard
I ran determined
Soon
The wind is behind me
Pushing me, driving me
I gain speed
I pass others
I am at the end
Winning
My hands rise in salute
I win
My life was not in vain
In the end I prevailed
It was the last lap
The final lap of life.

THE ANCIENT

I look around me
And see people
Vanishing behind modern sculptures
Enveloped in electronic gadgets
That hide their true identities
I stand alone
Surrounded by crowds
That I don't recognize
Faces and shadows
That seem alien
I realize
I am ancient
A creature of the past
That believes in love
Honesty, integrity, values and decency
Words that mean
Nothing to today's crowds
Ancient words that once had meaning
Today they are buzzwords
That people throw out
To flaunt their ignorance
I am ancient
For friendships are genuine
Not based on selfish self-interests
Honesty meant
True to oneself
Not just a word
That has lost its luster
Integrity implied respect
Not creating new meaning
Based on the situation

Values meant beliefs and convictions
That one stood on
Not justification for any action
Right and wrong
The world has changed
And I have not
I am still from the past
That believed in something
Today the world is different
Hollow and shallow
An empty void
That has no spirit
It is a world
I don't want
I'd rather be ancient
Than participate
In a society
That exists
Just to exist
I am old
I understand
The world has passed me by
I am left standing
On the oasis of the past
Alone
An ancient.

THE FINAL EXIT

We exit life
Many times in our lives
Seeking paths
That will lead us to the final exit
But, the final exit is final
It is the only exit that matters
For it is the end
The finality
When you don't have to worry about more exits
You have reached your destination
Whatever that maybe
Now you are free
At peace
And reflect on your journey
Was it good or bad?
Only God knows.

EXIT GRACEFULLY

The secret to a successful life
Is to exit gracefully
With dignity and self-respect
On your own terms
Not the terms
The world sets for you
It is your time
It is your precious moment
When you leave
The world of humans
For the kingdom of God
It is your shining moment
Time to shine like a bright star
In the dark sky
You are proud of what you have done
The best you can
You did it
Now, exit gracefully.

ABOUT THE AUTHOR

Dan Khanna considers himself a traveler through life enjoying an adventurous journey. Dan was born in New Delhi, India. After he completed high school, at St. Columbus High School, Dan left India striking out for California via short stays in London, Montreal and Milwaukee, Wisconsin. Although his dream was to pursue a career in the arts, acting, music, and writing, a quirk of fate placed him in engineering college and pursuing a business management career, in which he excelled. Dan completed an undergraduate program in engineering, and a Master and Doctorate in Business Administration.

Dan worked in Silicon Valley's high technology firms and was a CEO and founder of several firms. He changed careers to be a professor. Now, he again is pursuing his dream in creative endeavors.

Dan is the quintessential Renaissance Man, whose interests span the gamut of the arts, sciences, history, social and political studies, classics and philosophy. His search for knowledge began in his early life where his father was the Chief Education Officer of Delhi and his mother was a Sanskrit scholar. Dan speaks English, Hindi, Urdu, Punjabi, and Gujarati.

As a child, Dan read voraciously, particularly enjoying novels, such as Sherlock Holmes, Agatha Christie, Earl Stanley Gardener, Ian Fleming's James Bond series and classic works of Shakespeare, Tolstoy, Dickens, Oscar Wilde, Thomas Hardy, and other writers. He was very interested in poetry and read English poems of Browning, Keats, Milton, Tennyson, and Frost, as well as, other poets, while mastering Urdu poetry. His intellectual interests including studying Western and Eastern philosophers, especially Socrates, from whom he learned questioning methodology employed in his research, lectures and seminars.

During his parochial education, Dan was interested in various sports: cricket, soccer and field hockey. His love for the arts and music was honed to a level that he performed in plays, movies and solo concerts.

Dan's present journey is devoted to creative arts and activities, primarily writing poetry, fiction and non-fiction books and plays, while continuing to acquire knowledge of diverse subjects. He has published one book and has written over twelve hundred poems. Dan has several non-fiction and fiction books in development.